D0468485

At
the
Site
of
Inside
Out

At
the
Site
of
Inside
Out

Anna Rabinowitz

University of Massachusetts Press
Amherst

Copyright © 1997 by
Anna Rabinowitz
All rights reserved
Printed in the United States of America
LC 96–48655
ISBN 1-55849-092-2 (cloth) ; 093-0 (pbk.)
Designed by Sally Nichols
Set in Cheltenham
Printed and bound by Braun-Brumfield, Inc.
Library of Congress Cataloging-in-Publication Data

    Rabinowitz, Anna, date.
      At the site of inside out / Anna Rabinowitz.
        p. cm.
      Winner of the 1996 Juniper Prize.
      ISBN 1-55849-092-2 (alk. paper). —
        ISBN 1-55849-093-0 (pbk.: alk. paper)
      I. Title.
    PS3568.A238A9 1997   96–48655
    811' .54—dc21   CIP

British Library Cataloguing in Publication data are available.

Marty, always

Acknowledgments

Grateful acknowledgment is made to the following journals where these poems first appeared:

American Letters & Commentary, "Dislocations"
Black Warrior Review, "Mixed Media"
Caliban, "Lion, Sand, Moon, and You"
Colorado Review, "All Aboard Going Aboard"
Confrontation, "Art-Crazy Old Man"
The Cream City Review, "The Art of Painting"
Cumberland Poetry Review, "The Crossing"
Denver Quarterly, "Limited Visibility," "Again and Once Again
    and . . . ," "Ars Poetica"
Epoch, "Without"
George Washington Review, "Through the Motions"
Hampden-Sydney Poetry Review, "Deep Hems"
Mississippi Valley Review, "You Are Like This Where You Are"
Mudfish, "Tell Me a Story, as the Story Goes"
New York Quarterly, "Anatomy Lab"
New American Writing, "Of Two Minds"
The Paris Review, "Through Many Waters, Leaf-Light, the Tree"
Phoebe, "Below the Dome" appeared as "Abecedarium"
Poetry Northwest, "Of Pine"
San Francisco State University Review, "An Unbodied Joy Whose
    Race Has Just Begun"

Sonora Review, "Fragile Dialectics"
Southwest Review, "The Foreplay of Hermeneutics"
The Sow's Ear, "Lost and Found"
Sulfur, "Sappho Comments on an Exhibition of Expressionist
　Landscapes," "Descent," "Age"
Sycamore Review, "Linoleum Gardens" appeared as "Home"
1990 Quarterly, Summer, "Confession"

"Sappho Comments on An Exhibition of Expressionist Landscapes"
was reprinted in *The Best American Poetry 1989.*
"Top Knot" appeared in the anthology *Life on the Line: Selections on
Words and Healing,* Negative Capability Press, 1992.
"Anthem" and "Camera Work" appeared in the *1992 Roberts Writing
Awards Annual* and the *1993 Roberts Writing Awards Annual,*
respectively.

Special thanks to Jeanne Marie Beaumont, Suzanne Fox, Pearl London,
and Molly Peacock for believing in the work and for their unfailing, life-
enhancing support.

Contents

II

III

At
the
Site
of
Inside
Out

Below the Dome

About this they knew a lot, the old masters,
Brush by brick the blatant blare:
Chiaroscuro of cleft chins, crow-cadenced eyes,
Dramas dallying in valleys of silk cheek;
Elegies on steep hillsides:
Flaring clouds, fitful flesh,
Gabled, gnarled, gnostic markings
Holy as the highest,
Isolate as each living thing
Jolted to the enterprise, bent on
Knowing—
Language in the language of language—
Movement as the speech that does not lie,
Nature as the nostrum—bright-dark nemesis
Of past and present
Painting the painting of painting—
Query gone to quest gone to quote gone to quarrel with what is
Real in the ultimate
Scheme—if there is one—, asserting what they could,
Tit for tat, in the relentless
Unbuilding (rebuilding?) of this
Victimless superstructure, this
Wily, wave-battered, often
X-rated multitych
Yowling year after year for its
Zones.

I

Sappho Comments on an Exhibition
of Expressionist Landscapes

Then, she says, a penis is needed, female
artists almost always can use one, taking
charge with tools like brushes and palette knives to
        build up their pictures,

bold as men are, spraying great skeins of yellow,
cobalt blue, and crimson across the canvas,
rage or quiet made at their will, exploding
        measures of failure,

risking planes, dissolving full spaces, Bluemner
hurling turquoise clouds on a purple field as
blackbirds wheel in formation, Hartley sculpting
        skies out of granite,

oil as cloud made palpable, air as breathless
form accreting mass in its own defense while
ends begin and boundaries disappear.
        This is how men die.

Now, she says, O'Keeffe is my point, consigned to
desiccated bones smoother than silk, unblemished
petals, lilies swollen in heat, faint tensions
        vectored through tunnels,

warm vaginas, moisture of vulvas, furtive
stand-ins, meanings plain as your face: a woman
minus penis making art with her body,
        trapped in her body.

An Unbodied Joy Whose Race Has Just Begun

1.

Then I will fly solo to the bones of earliest memory
And I will revoke fields of sown obligation
I will demand a site-specific locale for the *face en face*
And I will disarm dialogue with splintered phrase
And I will needle Zeitgeist with parody
And I will backdate the check I'm to sign in the morning
And in the evening I will revise the beginning because its end is
     everywhere
Yes, I will plunder residues to state my case plainly
But I will be distant as the horn of the barreling car

So, where will you find me, where will you find me

2.

Yes, I will deliberate with the bones of earliest memory
And I will stow seed revoked from fields sown with obligation
And I will invent cosmic order for the *face en face*
And I will arm concept with splintered phrase
Yes, I will needle agenda with parody
And I will decode the check I'm to sign in the morning
And in the evening I will emulsify the beginning because the end is
     everywhere
Then I will plunder dream to state my case plainly
And I will be ambiguous as the distant horn of the barreling car

So, how will you find me, how will you find me

3.

Yes, I will fly solo to deliberate with the bones of earliest memory
And I will run rife with seed revoked from fields of sown obligation
And I will make actual a site-specific, cosmic order for the *face en face*
And I will disarm concept with the dialogue of splintered phrase
Yes, I will needle agenda with the Zeitgeist of parody
Then I will backdate the recurrent code of the vintage check I'm to
     sign in the morning
And in the evening I will revise the emulsified beginning beginning to end
And I will plunder dreamy residues to state my case plainly
And I will be beholder beheld, ambiguous as the strident warning of
     the distant horn of the barreling car

Try to find me, try to find me, try to find me

Lost and Found

The fact is the child did not need to learn about loss.
No one left because no one came.
When she wanted company, two ghosts
posed in a yellowed, deckle-edged
sepia blur spoke to her from a life
she knew nothing of.

One wore wool knickers and a peaked
cap. His eyes uttered faint pleas
against solitude. The other, a good deal older,
her face gridded with fine lines,
opened, closed her lips in elliptical
0's funneled through a fluted tongue.

The child had no recourse. Nothing ever changed
except the location of her desire, the frame
of her longing in which redress for the loss
of the knowledge of loss hunkered like a homeless dog.

There was a mother there lost in a loss quite real.
She had known those two though she barely
remembered. When she did she wrote fictions
with ragged syllables of memory: a splintered
bench, an oak table teetering of its own weight,
rose-budded oilcloth crazed in a chaos reminiscent
of fires that had raged out of everyone's control.
Sometimes she talked about a river sun-set
with diamond pavé, shadow cast on cursory
filaments of grass by the pointed roof
of the house, recalled how she could see through
everything, even those shadows as they sprawled there
struggling to be impenetrable. When she looked

with concentration her eyes had remarkable power.
A pebbled rise appeared, sheaves of grass spiraled
into the night to assert dominion over the plot, as if to reclaim
territory, as if to invoke a doctrine of landscape
transportable from place to place. But about those figures
she said: *this is my mother; he is my brother.* That was all.

The child focused on the image. She slipped
her arms into the sky draped behind them and wrapped
it around her body until she basked in their breaths.
She took the left hand of one, the right hand
of the other. Together they entered the world.

It was new, altogether different
from anything they had been familiar with.
They were not uneasy though there was
no path to direct them. They found no landmarks, no night.
They walked a white light, pure, clean, with a pencil
attached to one side. No one said a word,
not a single word, nor did any of them take
the pencil in hand to make a mark on that pristine
white they inched through, holding one another up
so as not to stumble in all that seeing, that white seeing.

There was much to be discovered. Everything
was there in that whiteness. All the colors,
all the nuances buried for eternities like ancient bronze
vessels, patinated with questions, overlaid
with answers. Or were they patinated to stir
the interest of scholars, collectors, exclamations
from the mouths of onlookers? They didn't want to know.

They had found each other. There was comfort in that.
And something natural, unwritten or erased, in not knowing.

The Foreplay of Hermeneutics

1.

From the top of her head to the black coagulation—
if you think she's floating you're right,
right over slippery scales of graphite.

From the top of her head to the black coagulation—
her throat slit by the hyphenated run.
If you think she's floating you're right,
right over slippery scales of graphite.

From the top of her head to the black coagulation—
her throat slit by the hyphenated run
impossible to subdue once begun.
If you think she's floating you're right,
right over slippery scales of graphite.

2.

Trust me. There's nothing unusual in a lost face.
Dismemberment gets to the parts (heart) of things:
what bleeds, what cannot; what seeps, what clings.

Trust me. There's nothing unusual in a lost face
severed between points, dismantled, erased.
Dismemberment gets to the parts (heart) of things:
what bleeds, what cannot; what seeps, what clings.

Trust me. There's nothing unusual in a lost face
severed between points, dismantled, erased,
flesh bone-dry or cloyingly moist, whatever the case.
Dismemberment gets to the parts (heart) of things:
what bleeds, what cannot; what seeps, what clings.

3.

Look, her lips couple with nuance ardent for things to say,
and under the text of her brow note how the eye,
spangled with lust, resets the margins of desire.

Look, her lips couple with nuance ardent for things to say
about hermeneutics parsed in foreplay
and under the text of her brow note how the eye,
spangled with lust, resets the margins of desire.

Look, her lips couple with nuance ardent for things to say
about hermeneutics parsed in foreplay,
language dandling codes fervently relayed,
and under the text of her brow note how the eye,
spangled with lust, resets the margins of desire.

4.

Adamant colors breathe deep, sustain your duress.
Eye, stick out your tongue. Shake up the old domain.
What is given to understand consorts on new terrain.

Adamant colors breathe deep, sustain your duress,
Fondle nails, ears, sweaty feet, punctuate each caress.
Eye, stick out your tongue. Shake up the old domain.
What is given to understand consorts on new terrain.

Adamant colors breathe deep, sustain your duress,
Fondle nails, ears, sweaty feet, punctuate each caress.
Lick the bottom of the bowl, sweet eye. Yes, oh yes,
Eye, stick out your tongue. Shake up the old domain.
What is given to understand consorts on new terrain.

Limited Visibility

Why, I ask myself, shouldn't the shining dots
of the sky be as accessible as the black dots
on the map of France?

                                    Vincent Van Gogh

1.

Dots for him on a dark page . . .
Will they rise on their haunches if the bristles mat?
What can they clutch if the brush stroke sweeps
them onto slippery terrain? On what pinnacle can they keep
their balance when the palette knife scoops them up?
Engined by benign indifference, will they rephrase shadows?

2.

By that time late afternoon had eroded the quicksilver
light of day, plunging him into the halftone
deceits that totter at the edge of landscape.
The minute hand had made its turn to the hour.
The location of its composure corresponded with the field
of vision compassed by his eyes. There was nowhere
else to go. A finality in that sweep, complete but unfulfilled,
made him unsure of where he was.

The shining dots pulsed thick and hot, circled the message.
Lacking specific goals, directional increments
were discrete but measurable like strolls among poplars.
Getting to know them would be like getting to know himself.

3.

Alien disembarked on a rooftop pocked

by jackhammers that sputter anxieties but draw no blood.
He voted to neutralize the background so it would not encumber him.
His intention was to express body, the mass of things, tenderness,
plasticity of flesh amidst ruggedness
for intimations of what had eluded him.
Gesture was everything.
Background would not serve as mediator.

4.

Do not fear death as locomotion.
Do not resist implacable demands
reduced to an understanding, each punctum cupped,
then examined by the hands of the mind.

Do not scour this landscape for wildlife or vegetation.
It wanders the long dark energy arranged by patterns.

Read the solitude flecked with dots as text
in the wilderness, a second way station
to the mystery. Definition is futile if desire
shifts one point in the proceedings.

Step out and walk around.

5.

At the horns of the dilemma: a pale circle with a deep center,
a break in the background reminiscent of an open mouth.
Tilted down, as if to pour out its contents, Aladdin's magic lamp.

But springboards are not the subject of the work.
The sun jitters in its space, splatters its raw
skin beyond the horizon and diverts his view.
The moon sleeps soundly on its side.
Black, white, and gray initiate the moment, but the spectrum
does not cool its heels. There is more to learn.

All Aboard Going Aboard

of all colors   the dense lore of them   the black border
hounds the white page   o the demands   on order
one two three   hide   in order   four five six   seek   land
where the hill breaks   where the shore cubes   the borderland
where looted harbors   where long ago   dolors of gold ore
refused to melt   ingot upon ingot loaded   full on board

how shall I bore into this   who has bored
out of this   please give up your cool   from where border
patrol forces have sped   I will not ignore clamors of language or
disguise myself   o the hooded roaming   in short order
the order to flee   the ports jammed   where the borderlands
why these doors   where the subject/subjects   where land–

ing holds its breath   on the spot   it is inscribed   we all land
together   we're in it together   o the fictions stored on board
"to think is to fail"   "in it together"   they sing no idea   borderlands
o resonant lanes   o corded woods   the weird boarders
whose untold parties   discarded rooms   numbing disorder
out of which   due to which   on stage   we must reor-

der   out of frayed shawls   erased disclosures   and/or
filthy fingernails   the palm roars in the mind   aborted land-
ings   where folklore shrieked to a halt   where the new order
silenced metaphor   where original lacunae climbed on board
where the temporary name themselves   where the border
takes its memory   where its pulse cannot be found   borderlands

what will it take   the opaque brittles   the night-baked borderland
where candors sprout from rocks   where characters cannot oar
out of estrangements   the darkling of that   will you get bored or
angry being neither here nor there   to have clawed to land
where fish are fowl   where it is not manageable   to be on board
hating the mirror and inking your face out of photos in order

to tell less than you know   where there is too much to order
where seams gape and hems weep   where sleeves moan   borderlands
where space is mute   where the volume is low   where board-
ed-up orifices mourn walls   of ships of state unmoored   of rumor
of absence   of digging   of plowing   of people   of no-one's land
of the tyranny of denial   of the monarchy of doubt   of the border

hoarding more borders   the record defiant with emptiness   of the order
to land before the final history   once and for all to the borderland
quick to the core   where first traces storm   all aboard   going aboard

Mixed Media

Bits and pieces

Butterflies—swallowtail, monarch, peacock—
fumbling for air, scales came off as dust
when he laid them in his palm,
worms, long lean omnivores he scooped
from coiled trails, glittering green
gargoyles of glass, buttons, beads,
the false jewels . . .

Excavations from lost civilizations

From drawers, pockets, from the corners
of deeds, he gathered fistfuls of Cracker Jack charms,
bobbins, cloud-flecked marbles, the core of an apple,
Five & Dime rings, a nosegay of needles,
even the blood of a wounded sparrow became in his hand
a rare ruby to set with the rest on the tesselate landscape.

Trying to get a hold on things

Perhaps he said, "I will need these things,"
his longings precise properties
of what he could possess and repossess.
Perhaps he harvested scattered reflections
of himself, migrated hundreds,
even thousands of miles over ocean and mountain
to find quiet at the heart of disarray.

The story is told not by telling but by going on

He sought order in a grid of wool skeins,
the braid of twigs, bundled shreds of paper,
then sank his toes into shifting sands, filled the air
sacs of his hollow bones with the language

of call notes to chirr the pleasure and the pain.
If I enter the nest of his collections,
will I find him there,
eyes wide, a furrow between his brows,
also saved?

for my father Sam Goldban (1902–1986)

Of Two Minds

What if we were to say, yes, there is a purpose,
plangent, numinous, even palpable, but not known to the mind,
there is a place, identifiable as your face, for this purpose,
also an hour, say 12 noon or 5 p.m., for the purpose,
unassailable as the rock of our despair?
Suppose we were propelled here to discover the purpose
by a fidelity composed of its own intractable purpose
and, as moths dote on stars—bloated with desire—
we were to grope endlessly through caves paved with desire
(or could it be need?) to believe, yes to believe, in this purpose
not only now or then but for the sake (in the name) of all time,
particularly because all we have in the end is time?

What if we were to agree for all things there is a clock marking time,
minutes in disarray, trembling, longing for order, and hands of purpose
to sack then mend, set, reset, flail fists in the air, press palms in due time
to arrest the present—to fix eyes on the main topic when time's
cradle stills the unborn child and an old woman, humming in her mind
of bare branches, bears in mind that waves alter sandbars each time
they cruise (smash) over them, that curled tongues of water slam time
and again against kelp, gnash teeth into seaweed, driftwood, paring
down their intrusions, how, though the wind bullies, then ravels despair
into bubbling selvages, water finds its level every time,
that even the shore, suckling the late light, contending, husky with desire,
girds its shoulders, beats its breast, but cannot outwit the sea's desire?

Tell me, then, why this gentle tyranny at center stage—this woman
      who crops desire
between two thighs of cloth, her needle stitching—slowly stitching—
      hyphens in time?
Tethered to the brittle death of withered flesh, for her no showstopping
      bows to desire,
no denouement quoting clouds, no plot hidden in the deep hems of
      desire.
Being-in-the-world—cheek by jowl—tick by tock—to what purpose

should she ache to shape wholes of parts, fruit of seed, the glass of desire
clouded, crazed, raised to her lips, on her tongue the sweet cream of desire?
On frail legs how does she scale cratered recollections that loom in the mind,
emptinesses seeking names, the interminable sentence springing to
      mind,
concentric layers spinning like rings around the heart of a tree's desire?—
(Hold on—for dear life—hold on, make it yours—you will be reeled in
      [in despair?],
[as enactment?] [by artifice?] sucked up by the eye of your fate—
      but do not despair.)

Everything—(do you hear this?)—there is everything here to spare,
but she nears the millennium and the closed (flung open?) door
      unspent by desire
but unwilling, the thought of never-having-been her secret rock of despair—
this aged, paltry thing who knows not how to be invisible, why to prepare—
pianissimo—to step out of the way—though it is time—(hurry up, please)—
      it's time
not to know where to go from here, time now in a cold season to slip into
      prayer—
oh, lord—to pray for a foothold in the loneliness, not to plunge to despair
but to finish the narrative with the ease of a finch lighting down, as if the
      purpose
is to perch somewhere or to float rather than sink, to keep studding purpose
with the cloves of unanswered cries, the snowy stutterings of despair
as rime on wide fields of sky, the stumbling footprints of sheep reminder
(reminiscence?) of how all these years she's believed it a case of mind

over matter to seek change, to scratch notches in the surface, to read the
      mind
of the story when verbs rise on their haunches, and nouns, threatened,
      despair
of their names. There is comfort in linear events, in marching in place,
      peace of mind
in the taut skin of routine—no might-have-beens, no what-ifs, no whys to
      jar the mind,
or mar the scene. This is about a strict obedience, a political correctness
      that sets desire

against happiness (contentment?) (resignation?). This, in truth, is about
   a small mind,
focused, some might say, on simple business—inhale, exhale—with time
   to kill—a mind
determined to stick it out with feathers unruffled. Well groomed, this mind
   at almost any time
of day, making room for itself, not able to read the small print, taking
   one step at a time
into the nothingness which may be something, which may be meant to
   crowd the mind's
court. Does she see into it (out of it?) (without it?)? None of the above.
   Forget purpose.
Let her keep her house in order, her clothes wrapped in tissue paper
   absent of purpose.

Let her arrange, rearrange goldenrod, daisies, gomphrena, sleep and
   wake for the purpose
of three meals on schedule, rainfall, birdcall, a stroll across the lawn,
   paying no mind
to codas or the air roiling in the heat of late August—stranger to despair,
on her lips—(does she taste it?)—an insatiable need granulating (or is it
   desire?)
pertaining to gold—a wound healing—a plea without reply—it's time—
   high time.

Fragile Dialectics

A chessboard floats
      between two old men
           armpit deep in the pool.
One fat man's veins
    clog with layers
of cholesterol.
           In the prostate of the other
    a small node
      accretes cells rapidly.
    Their fingers,
thick at the knuckles,
           bend into arcs and angles,
      kings, queens, pawns
within boundaries.

Two women finger the fans of their cards.
     The blonde's bones soften
             at the base of her spine where
       she feels a faint, pulsing ache.
The redhead's skull is inlaid with a metal plate
     the size of a three-by-five index card.
She feels vaguely cool
            despite the weight of her wig.
     They shuffle, deal, play their hands,
    deuces wild,
beneath the lid of the clock.

At a nearby table a man and a woman
eat their lunch.
       Her colon has been amputated.
   His atrium fibrillates.
             Her abdomen rounds.
       His scrotum rests
in the cove of his crotch.

At the borders of their temples,
above their lips,
among their pubic hairs
tiny beads of moisture swell.
It is noon, mid-August.
They cut their food.

Reading the Newspaper
While Trying to Write a Poem

Released data tell us that
despite all attempts
to deny the fact,
we have failed to cut it.
Our children read less,
add and subtract like
lame birds with clipped
wings on the lam, marry
late, then father and mother
fatherless, motherless
offspring because they work
all day, spend an hour in the
gym each a.m., attend dinner,
theater, etc. at night.

Vagrants warble the blues,
then passionately,
with decision, twist
screwdrivers, jab
blades into the smooth,
lovely, ringleted shoulders,
the taut stomachs, the pink-
nippled chests of unsuspecting
joggers, of dog walkers
rinsing their faces in new-dawn
sun, strollers coasting

like dancers—slow, quick,
quick—to this fox-trot/
waltz/tarantella called life.

Clashes serrate the veins
of breakaway republics,
the volcano pelts its spewed-
out parol into the crowd of
nineteen-year-old males
on the make, and men
and women of all ages
take turns lying on the
rumpled white sheet while
the psychic healer, gone
twenty years now
from New Zealand, warms
their skulls with the heat
of his knuckles,
the sweat of his palms.

And the only news
under the sun is my mother,
now nothing and nobody's
business, still true as a plumb
line from the masthead
to the end of the page.

Confession

Perhaps I should let you in
on the time I threw a knife
at my brother.

Neither of us remembers
what made me do it, why him
as the target,

why me on the offensive
trying to get something out
of my system,

just that I was mad as hell,
the blade gleamed on the table,
and he was there.

Through Many Waters, Leaf-Light, the Tree

Drones out brittle, weary invocations, the certainty of fruit
                                    now distant as the first word
On God's tongue. Such disarray. So much leaf-rot, leaf-loss,
                                    leaf-ache heaped up. No
Petiole, no rib, no vein, no heart unscathed by knowledge of its
                                    plight. Apprenticed to a sleep
Purged of epoch, a region seasoned with what remains unnamed
                                    when alphabets crowd up
Earth-logged, victims of predictable defection. No word, no phrase
                                    avails (exists?) to make whole
Language which drops everything soon or late while we try to
                                    beat back decay like mongrel
Ghosts of fleshly (fleshless?) selves. Out of enclosure. Into enclo-
                                    sure. Mouthing our lines. Straining
After meaning. This rabble of leaves, these mute trees. And this
                                    late-leaning, fast-fading appoggiatura
Narrowing down to prayer beside a blue window. The familiar
                                    after-feeling peers in,
Gazes out. Alter ego, friend or foe, our deepest wish lies on the
                                    other side of the bog
Eternitied to might-have-been. What can I do, where can I go?
                                    Whether I run or stand stock-still, no tongue
Restrains this next life as it passes into your eye, this last silence
                                    as it oceans to your ear.

for Marilyn Bergner (1933–1992)

The Art of Painting

In the room, tapestry, velour, a Roman mask,
a volume open on the table, two chairs
braided and fringed, a brass chandelier
needing to be lit
before the sun goes down.

The woman does not play her trumpet
or read the book cradled in her arm.
She stands there draped in blue silk,
dwarfed by the map
nailed to the wall.

The coastline swells near her mouth,
hills rise at her brows, the line of her nose
echoes spires and towers of towns
in medallions to left and to right.
Her skin, smooth as the sea,
fills with ships set to sail

or headed for port.

Deep Hems

This is not about marginal trimming,
nor enclosure, nor the doubled over
enterprise of foldup, fold down,
not boxed-in pleats or a border
one deletes at the site of inside out.

Let grass stand at attention.
Let the mountain screw its spine into the sky.
Let the house clutch its stubble of ground,
and the bridge redouble its effort to fly
across boundaries, scuttle through doubt.

What we've got here is faith:
knees open to receive,
knees fisted into the future,
knees abandoned to the upswirling belief
that, firm or shriveled, one thing is sure:

we're bent to disclose what really counts:
below the knee, at the knee, an inch or two
above—anything goes. Lines redrawn,
lengths easily altered, the view
leaps from the bridge as it laps at the sun.

Linoleum Gardens

1.

When I try to go by land   breaking out of the distance
the shadow-hunched streets   are all the same
I probe   caves of doorways
alleys   bleary windows   roam the spoor
trolley tracks   under the el   seeking a sign

Then   yesterday   I recalled Gravesend Bay
when I thought about going home   of being drawn to hills
to open plains   even to places like Brooklyn   where available light
is no more than a slice   of the blue obligation
the sky had that winter of '83

2.

I am not a strong swimmer   I enter the waters   slowly   naked
as when I first appeared to you   in the silence   when sound
is called into being   It is a huge silence   the bones of my life in it
and the waves   untangling   unsnarling
pitch me to shore   steps from where you were alive

For the first time   I see you in full light
shielding your eyes from the glare   (I remember
you did not want your face   its eyes   buried cribs
cradled a longing you could not define)

You stand at the porcelain sink   between its bulbous legs
at the stove   to ladle scum   from the broth
at the window   to shake crumbs
down the narrow shaft   You kneel with a damp rag
to scour scuffs   persistent as weeds
from your linoleum garden

The tiny yard behind the house has grown wild   roses, dahlias
crouch on their stems   gnarl with vines into a crippled
matwork of sprawl   paint on the picket fence   curls
to a carnage of flakes   on the clothesline
muslin sheets   stiffen in the sun

3.

Time after time   I said you stole away from me

but it was I   who swam in the wrong direction
cropped by jetties   neglected opportunities
to know you   when you lasted   more than an image or two

In this moment   what arrangement   can I make
of a few phrases of light glazing my eyes   what language
repairs   this grammar of relic   stumbling   to your shore

for my mother Ruth Chernoff Goldban (1902–1983)

Anthem

Let us praise appropriate images—tadpoles that father assemblage in
the flea market of the city's debris.
Let us praise cast-off elements—weeds of hair curled on the barbershop
floor, the glitter, then rust of bottle caps, the green vessels,
the brown.
Let us praise Styrofoam cups, chipped plates, the crush of cardboard
cartons, yellowed newsprint descended nude into public
squares.
Let us praise emulsions—cold creams, make-up bases, shaving foams—
and the jars, the aerosol props in which they formulated
their aesthetic of truth.
Let us praise spent tubes of Neosporin, sun block, Vaseline, the foggy
declarations of broken glass, mirrors emptied of reflection
and desire.
Let us praise unloosed wires—telephone, electric, TV cables, wire gauge,
wire gauze of the ink-laden screen.
Let us praise billboards with rubbed out words, labels spewed by tin
cans, mosaics of rag sprawled in central malls, the marbles,
ribbons, weary yarns.
Let us praise tables with broken legs, split broomsticks, chairs with
warped seats, the dwindling narrative of sofas revoking their
Dacron guts.
Let us praise threadbare rugs, unknotted tufts, loop and cut pile murals
shunted from warp and weft to bear witness in the yard
sales of round afternoons.
Let us praise frayed braid, cords, hooks, steel eyes, zippers lacking
teeth, the bone buttons, the untied bows.
Let us praise hybrid pieces. They have moved like squeegees across the
scrims of our lives, through impastoed passages.
Let us praise minimalizing urges, the remains, the residues, the marginal—

Because they are connected to origins, because they codify our movement,
Because they are context and collage, icon and diehard, push and pull,
conceived and holding on.

II

Tell Me a Story, as the Story Goes

With nights lengthening, there was time to consider the language
of pages and places, how, ambitious for order, it fenced in the borders
of life, kept events in tow, corralled her story
that would be told and retold to anyone with the habit
of listening, anyone who would be a squatter
inside the episodes, engrossed, leaning on his elbows

in the dusk, asking questions, even laughing, elbowing
her from the corners of memory, making her prod language
out of the concern which burgeons when a squatter
arrives on another's turf, is attentive, doesn't get tired, or bored, or
start to roam in his own history, slave to the common habit
humans have, though companionable, of living out only the personal story.

One afternoon, in the rain, someone came. He climbed up six stories
to be with her, to share coffee, under the rainbow
of her recollection where consonants, shifty vowels inhabit
lifetimes no matter how brief, poor, or abandoned by language,
no matter how uncertain our knowledge of the borders
of understanding, because, let's face it, he said, we're all squatters

in the desert, on fields, in woods, we are squatters
who casually slip into the robe of the same story,
let folds of fabric fall around the borders
of our bodies, around our necks, down our arms, past elbows
of desire to familiar ground where language
reminds us we stand erect with opposable thumbs, clothed in habit

that prevails regardless of fashion, much as nuns in their habits,
at ease, spread their skirts, kneel, even squat
before things not given to them to understand, beyond the language
of reason, committed to faith, while, relentlessly, history
goes on repeating itself as if it had never happened before, elbowing
everything along the way into exile within borders.

Then, even faith, she said, doesn't go free. It has its border
patrols to demand passports, visas, evidence of all the habits
designed to keep us in check, on our toes and off our elbows,
as if we'd be fool enough in this place to think we're not squatters
who ask certainty of doubt, each of us stalking a unique story
to scrawl all over the pages of a book written in a language

we labor to recall. Still, borders can be crossed by squatters
like us. Come, let us husband our habits in order to trap the story
which, she said, elbows, yes, elbows its way to the language.

Dislocations

I. Renegade Tide

Tuesday, May 9, a meeting in the lounge, Moskva Hotel, Leningrad

Chairs split
cotton batting   springs
muscle   out of confinement

Vladimir   almost twenty
pursed lips   lean
against yellow   twisted   teeth

His father's mouth   four roots
and their enamel   long gone
from the upper gum
Lower teeth   swivel left   right

I sit on a sprung sofa
with two Refuseniks   accused
of access to state secrets
eleven years ago

The father   then   day after day   riveting
metal in a munitions plant   The son   then
day after day   carrying her books   luring
Natalia   behind the ancient oak
for a soggy   eyeflash kiss

My teeth grind grit
Knotted jaws square
the corners of my face

How much longer must they wait
for the noose of one room
to loosen
for necks to glisten in new rain
to break out   to fly
200 rubles in their pockets   diamonds in their eyes

Our room overlooks the Bay of Finland where a wide sky today forgets its blue. On broad boulevards, people walk, deliberate as clenched teeth, peer into empty shop windows, sprint to join queues, wait for May 20, some say, when the fountains go on at Petrodvorets and things will change.

Wednesday, May 10, noon, Marat Street

Irina   In this country
everyone lies   even the ants

There are three ants
one   two   three
all in a row
then one here   two in front
now two here   two behind

How can that be

Answer   one ant lies

Each person has his secret lie
sweltering in the heat of his swollen chest
his open lie skulking in the corner of his eye
his wounded lie parsing truth where his mouth used to rest

Guaranteed   SILENCE

Thursday, May 11, Moscow

What is true in this city scored with crenelation
where Stalin spires jab the air and a spiral stair
leads us to a balcony overlooking Red Square

       Everywhere bulbous-legged women, metal-toothed men, pavement cracking beneath their feet. Marble steps contour to relentless treads, walls repeal paint in small particles.
       Our guide asks if writing starts with an idea.

People-clotted streets   stop   start   again   again
three for one   seven for one   thirteen for one
dollars   francs   marks   Switzerland   Germany
tough hard currency
to drive out the bad

       And the lie

Young men sell cash   seats for the Bolshoi   parterre
orchestra   below cost   tonight's performance   anywhere
any time   any day   anything   for dollars

       Our knot-hard   fist-clenched   boot-heel currency

Friday, May 12, apartment of book designer Natasha Kadushin

Books pop open   a fish rounds
his mouth   snakes uncoil   the lion snarls
On the table   baked pigeons   caviar
white and walnut-tinted breads
shredded butter   wine-dark tomatoes
border of braised leek   potatoes
basted with parsley threads

Natasha's smile   gums show
square teeth
between spaces

Like the gaps in reality

The samovar beads sweat on its brass skin
between pages   the rabbit leaps

What is the angle
Who knows the lie

Follow the ants

Saturday, May 13, supper, home of Yevgeny Kagan

We drink a champagne toast
circling a bowl of giant strawberries
mocha cream cake   sugar-drizzled cookies
The famous filmmaker is our host

One hundred women line up for eggs on Gorky Street
two hundred for sugar on Arbat   Where is the meat

What is the meat
Dog   Horse   Beef

Sunday, May 14, in and around GUM

Obligation   obbligato
When in Russia   hustle   rummage
stalk the turn   shoot the curve
scavenge the back counter

Sleuth us each day our daily bread

II. Boundaries within Stone

Monday, May 15, 11 a.m., Prague

Rash gazer wipe your eye

Shoulder to shoulder trees clamor
down the hills across the Charles Bridge   over
the Vlatava   past the statue of the Rebbe from Lvov
a naked woman   crawling up his side
death   they say   in disguise
to the astronomical clock in the Old Town Square
where the Jew of painted wood   emerges   each hour
through a secret door   holding his sack of gold
or is it stones   or the bones
of his forefathers   or the rags
of his hope   the nails in his heart
the scorched wing
of his longing

> *Hickory   dickory   dock*
> *The Jew peers from the clock*
> *The clock strikes one*
>
> *The Jew   What has he done*
> *Hickory   dickory   dock*

Beautiful Prague   sun scalds the finials of St. Nicholas
sears stone blocks in the square
drowns the faces of buildings
What lies behind the lilts and curves

> *The dissident writer is jailed for nine months*

Blue day   yellow day
The door opens   wood puckers
tears inch down the hinges
Like oil they anoint the ancient tarnished brass

Nothing could keep the children from remembering their homes, toys, the dishes for their food, how they skated across square ponds or carried baskets of fruit on the carousel. But some, like Eva Mettnerova, drew black pitchers, black daisies, scattered leaves of soot through the sky.

At last we are in a clean hotel and the water is drinkable.

Wednesday, May 17, the old Jewish ghetto

> *Thy root is ever in its grave*
> *And thou must die*

The cemetery   buck   gnarl   twist
earth weighted with our deaths
choked within boundaries   bridling

> *So we blanketed the fits and starts*
> *New soil   New flesh   New stones*
> *Over   now   over*

Rabbi Loew's tomb   Wishes
inserted in crevices
rear   among cobwebs

> *Golem Recipe*
> *One kilo mountain soil*
> *One litre spring water*
> *Knead with heel of right palm*
> *Yields one servant   YHWH*
> *Sealed between his eyes*
> *Beware   When he runs amok*
> *Peel the letters from his brow*

Relentless candor of decay
sprays of ivy   claw stone

Tier upon tier   plies of experience
The dead lie   disturbed

Even stones   grow weak   helpless
tilt   bend   erode   press
against each other
but not forever

Thursday, May 18, the study of the 16th-century Jewish Town Hall

The Cantor rocks on his stool   In Yiddish
Everything   we have everything   money   food
clothing   enough books   roofs over our heads
and prayers   *taleisim   yarmulkes*   but of people
we are poor   poorer than mice in barren fields

The Rabbi   clutches the arms of a threadbare chair
Let us seal the pockets of our eyes
Let us empty the sleeves of our ears
Let us not make problems

Rise dead   shake dirt from your teeth
brush flakes from your bones
bind the threads of your muscles
throw fists of worms to the wind
Stones hold your breath   Mark this time

III. Purple Blood of Lilac

Among the Technicians there were two schools of thought: the classic and the modern: the firing squad at twelve paces or the simple bullet plunged into the back of the neck from less than a meter's distance. The latter method won out because it was deemed more efficient and because it avoided confrontation with mortal distinctions of face. This led, however, to a period in which necks were on everyone's tongue, in everyone's thoughts—necks, corridors of necks, tunnels paved with necks, some dotted with pocks, blackheads, others rivered with fine blue veins, creased necks, necks tussocked with hair, depressed here and there by serial folds, neck upon neck, neck to neck gleaming with sweat, the concatenation of skin tones ranging from blush pink to soiled beige, even once in a while a tanned neck. And these necks gathered in the dreams of the Technicians, making them uneasy during the heretofore peaceful hours of their nightly sleep.

This gave impetus to the discovery and perfection of the use of gas as the means to make the world *Judenrein* . . .

Friday, May 19, International Hotel, Cracow

I have come to visit the family graves
where they may have been   the places

I nod as he tells me I cannot understand
How does one say cry in Yiddish
How does one say howl
How does one *know*   when one hasn't witnessed
father kill son   son father   for a piece of bread

> *We tell you with our own eyes*
> *we have seen such things in Auschwitz*
> *that could not happen on this planet*

**Saturday, May 20, dinner with a tour group from Israel in the hotel
restaurant**

Survivors   read poems   discuss the Talmud
sing   Polish   Hebrew   Yiddish

> *Welcome   we are all Jews*
> *Crawl into our eyes*
> *They hoard what we remember*

Poland   you are the largest graveyard in the world

Under the chestnut trees

under the oaks
under the trolley tracks   under the unkempt grass
under the pavement where *Ulica Wotynska*
turned to powder
under the monument at *Umshlagplatz*

> *where they rounded us up   on the corners*
> *where we talked   beside the manhole cover*
> *where as children we skittered like frantic mice*
> *in and out of the ghetto   to steal*
> *potatoes   radishes   a few limp carrots*

> *How many of us   lifting the steel cap   got a barrel*
> *between the eyes   in the back of the skull*
> *through the heart   scurrying legs   wing-light feet*
> *arms of shattered glass   splatter of gravel on cobbled streets*

One egg   two eggs   three eggs
pocket full of eggs
mouth full of broken teeth

Sunday, May 21, Auschwitz/Oswiecim

I am voyeur   interloper
sculptor
of statistic
collater
of relic

> *Poland 1939*
> *grandparents seated on a bench*
> *about the rest*
> *a window   ajar*
> *leans   against the shutter*
> *the sill   tilts*
> *a pot of violets   oddly bent*
> *their feet   out of focus*
> *breaking into rubble*

Hairworks   assemblage of matted strands
abhorrent province of haircloth
Wireworks   spectacles gnarled
among charred lenses

Crate of gold teeth

Where are the heads
the Polish guide
asks   then   replies
In Heaven

Where is my grandmother's enamel washbasin
the pitcher for warm milk
where grandpa's *talis*   their names on the rosters
surname   given name   *Jude*   birthdate   place of birth

We pass farmlands
women rake the grass
dust of green wire
rust   on rocking fields
close by   the rails

Monday, May 22, Brok

The river you swam   filled with sludge
the trees you climbed   scrub and weed
In these streets women wear short pleated skirts
teased hair   on their arms   plastic shopping bags

Your stories   Were they true

> *Today I saw four women wearing babushkas*
> *Only one would have known she was sporting an old style*
> *Old as the photo of my Polish grandmother*
> *sitting on the bench in front of her house*
> *Everything comes back*
> *even the dead*

Tuesday, May 23, Treblinka

Wide quiet of pine
in spring embroidered with sun
in winter rimed with white crystals
jeweled sentinels   alabaster crowned

Oh   earth   you are so beautiful

Terrace of railroad ties leads
to *Himmelweg*   Between the planks
weeds lunge from fertile soil
No blots of char   no bones
bleached by sun   no teeth
to mulch the rolling fields

Wednesday, May 24, Ostrolenka

Mama   there is no proof
The town hall has nothing to say
nor does the cinder block building
standing where your frame house may have been
nor the porch where young men guzzle shade with cold beer
I have asked the babushka'd women
the toothless kitchen gardener

Where is the quarter where the Jew people lived

Far-off   the million greens of early spring
chestnuts bloom   clustered triangles
of lavender and white probe the sky
on the road hoof falls of an old horse
pulling a wooden wagon
At the Narew's edge a festoon of foam
ruff around the creped neck of wild grass

One day I flushed
a rail from the reeds
and found in him something familiar
when he darted from the marsh and tried to fly
He was reluctant
his legs dangled down

Because I failed
to get the story from my parents   if they knew it

Because I wanted to make palpable
to reinvent what was   or   may have been
Because   because

Even of them what do I know
Arch of brow   downward slope of mouth
crackleware of thin skin below deep-set eyes

Leave the past to itself
Let it crouch in the corner of the room
or loom now bright now vague
behind the eyelid of the mind

Leave it
There is no sequel
no facsimile

Leave them where they are
They are not lonely there

Thursday, May 25, Warsaw

At the concert in Lazienki Park hundreds congregate around the pond where a bronze tree cradles Chopin. A prize-winning pianist performs the Heroic Polonaise in A flat. Not far away a plaque: "We do not know why we have been removed from this place, but we know who will play the Funeral March."

46

I have seen the places where they were
snapped them with my Olympus   shot the street signs
the muddy waters of the Bug   focused on crumbs in the parlor of the baker
who remembered only that he knew of them   that they went away
They lived in the heart of the town   beside his church
They were poor   poor Jews

> *Poor Jews   Problem solved*
> *Gone   gone   bone in the throat*

So many naked hips touching   in one place
air heated   arms thrust to heaven   poison pellets
swilled by warm moist molecules

> *WHO CAN IMAGINE THAT*

Did they look like flares in the distance
uncoded messages in the dark
received without reproach or denial

IV. Continental Drift

Friday, May 26, Kennedy Airport, New York City

It is the month of *Sivan,* a time when history ferments in bruised
casks, the juice of grapes, currants running mud-black. The sky crowds with
yellow stars. Fingerless fists pound on bolted doors. Large bones of the
foot—*talus, cuboid*—resistant to flame, ford the riverbanks.

Among recycled fumes
Sara   the *zogerin*
the sayer   importuner
of the dead and of God
a kerchief on her head
face shriveled

color of sand
darts like sand frisked
by the wind
lips   fluent with grammar   discharged
for the townspeople   for the strangers
who await the chant of syllables

> *She knows what to do   what to shout*

At her words   tombstones cringe
the dead shift their weight

> *I have advanced by comma and hyphen*
> *down a route made longer by ignorance*
> *The confused generations are parched leaves*
> *mingled with the past in throngs of stone*

Good morning   Rivke
good morning   Rokhl   Simkha   Yossel
all of you   sealed in your convoys
good morning

How can you lie peacefully
Your children and grandchildren need you
Exert yourselves   for their sakes
Call out to the Lord of the Universe
You know where to find Him   better than we do
You have rested enough   Action   Action

He has said He will come to us   if we listen
to His voice   But when we listen we hear
the center of silence

Weather rattles in our lungs

You are in charge here
Call out   Call out

> *CALL OUT*

III

Through the Motions

after Paul Taylor

It is winter. The orchestra scrambles scales
as dancers stream from the piano into the corner suite.
They glide to the esplanade paved with grasses of yesterday.

While the snow is still white, it is neat
to minor in the past where the future cloaks major chords
in the velvet robes of Byzantium and figures facing east

wage spells with runes pried from the secret scores.
They lie on the sorcerer's sofa, palms turned from God,
bodies like cooled coals in the aftermath of noon glare.

At sunset, when the sky fills its hods
with random apostrophes of cast-off blue and the clash-
dash of black fluencies, when organza-clad

women cascade into the arms of rash
suitors, will brasses playing an untitled serenade
forestall tomorrow with its decipherable message?

Will heroes, heroines, whispering in tongues, arrayed
as jagged chins speared forward in measures of defiance,
knees coterminous with the front lines, or gnarled braids

of leg, arm, torso counterswarm for a Maypole dance
and the mercuric tidings of ambivalent dream?
Will there be time for regrouping on the off-chance

that bolted doors and draped windows are not what is claimed?
The house of cards totters and falls. Breathless,
they carry each other, crawl, grope head to beam

while the spindle they dance unweaves mesh,
and music dispenses memories of tap-root flesh.

Ars Poetica

1.

One way to keep ideas, alphabets, even images flowing between
Two distant bodies is to work with a number. In this case, I'd opt for
Three: A and B, who speak across oceans, and C, the energy they share.
Four is too prone to predictable symmetries based on one and two;
Five traps what is singular between indifferent duos of higher integers;
Six divides into doubles, then triples to obfuscate activities in negative
      space;
Seven burdens the slim rod of one with two threesomes when one would
      suffice;
Eight places these trios on either side of a duality to crowd the arena
      with foreshadowings of
Nine—three x three—similar to what we began with, but redundant. And
      forget
Zero. It's bound to drive us crazy—circling, forever circling, stalking
      a center or close.

2.

Alphabets act with agility
Before assonance, alliteration,
Consonance, anaphora or other
Devices dramatize a dilemma
Equal to our very existence.
Few of us find fault in
Grammars geared to
Hieroglyphs and hortatory
Incantations composed of
Juxtapositions of
Knowledge-based,
Language-driven,
Meaning-ridden
Notations that claim to

Organize our thinking.
Perhaps we're
Quite within our
Rights (rites?) when each
Salutation
Ticks off a particular thing, known or
Unknown. Perhaps the
Very thought of a new approach to
Words threatens us with being
Xed out, exiled from
Yesteryears and yesterdays, from
Zeroing in on A to Zed the same old way.

3.

Let us wander, you and I, through the language of mystical value
Where characters, like butterflies, emerge from count-down cocoons
Into the sapphire environs of an uncoded mis en scene.

>   *A ship sails into port*
>   *Laden with diffused sunlight*
>   *and thoroughly drenched pots.*

Certain things are fundamental to all special needs:
Abundant growth and dawn sitting in a bowl of water.

for Lynda Sandhaus

Art-Crazy Old Man

Even as a ghost
My spirit will want to roam
The fields of summer.

Hokusai

Demanding there be no shadow,
no wake to the racing line,
he flew,
place to place, 93 times,
flew on his pots of paint,
in his garrulous hands
brushes, paper,
flew, body of wind,
borer into secret things, in dread
of leaving merely a blot,
with pigment strings bound the passing world—
cranes, herons flushed from the reeds,
rain, sparrows swept to a wind-tossed hat,
geishas at rest, elbows bent, toes ardently curled.

Descent

. . . then I began to think it would help my expression to have her descending.

Marcel Duchamp

She was supposed to be ascending, but who cares
to see a woman going up if given the choice.
Let her cascade down the winding stairs

    looking like dynamite-riven armor or worse:
    a julienne of skived leather, perhaps, a crush of tin,
    the aftermath of an earthquake, an accordion coerced

        to unfold, a swagger of broken violins
        deprived of their tone, a house coming down,
        shingles splintered, a nude with an affliction

            of shingles coming down, a shingle factory coming down,
            or, better yet, explosion of the shingle factory.
            Or is she a man? Or disguised as a man

                out to prove she won't be known easily,
                or that, broken into planes, she's a presence
                who can make it with or without the stairway,

                    up or down if she wishes, wherever she is.
                    Sequential, analytic, machinelike or not,
                    guyed as a hoax or revered as a goddess,

                        she makes the future bend to her strut.
                        This kind of woman troops down to step out.

The Crossing

She meant to change the world.
Yes, in a blizzard of syllables her boat
lunged through frenzied waters, provinces unfurled
by demeanors of foam and wave, remote

from domestic regions where so far she'd been in tow.
During star-struck nights and sunburned
days, she wrote:
"At last I have learned

I must enter the center of my name. There I will earn
my keep on this planet, there
my will can turn
to shore to repair

the splintered hull of my gender.
I will bear no child.
I will be no pretender
on the coasts of equality, nor will I be filed

away, inventoried in the hold
at your dayless port.
I will not grow old
having only cooked and cleaned. Do not court

me to cavort in your bed as dessert
for your hunger, to serve meals on cue,
to brook silence with fear, to skirt
my thighs, bind my waist with aspects of you.

I will not get my due
or settle my score with life
by being second to you
or any man.
          Be well.
                    Your loving wife."

These, my mother's words, tell half
the story. The other half goes like this:
She had two kids, said, "Enough, enough,"
but waited on him hand and foot as if his

survival and hers depended on it. She lost
herself in needlework, each household chore,
and an occasional matinee, and when she crossed
over this second time spoke no words to name her shore.

Top Knot

Because life is short she learned how to live with things, took them in as if they were waifs at her doorstep and offered them haven.

I found her in the master bedroom divested of props—her fitted dress, the turban that covered her skull. And it was O.K.—a split second jolt, then a quick accommodation.

She looked better, I thought. Her robe fell far enough from her body to conceal how thin she'd become. Her head looked strange but interesting, divided like the map of an irregular landscape—half a dozen territories exposed without modification by the shrill sunlight that plunged into the room—each area a different color—a deep pink over her left eye, pale off-white above the nape of her neck, gray over the temples, even a few islands of skin echoing the marmoreal tones of her face. The boundaries swelled slightly as if cord had been laced under her skull in strategic places, the way markers or dividers are set up between borders.

And crowning the hairless expanse, rising from the modest ridge of her brows, a mound, a top knot of skin the surgeon had gathered, shaped, and stitched into a bun.

Out of frustration, she said, and ingenuity.

Since she imagined he had always wanted to model in clay or stone, what else to do but use the materials at hand?

for Joan Sovern (1936–1993)

Anatomy Lab

Cut off the breasts,
examine them carefully,
then pass them around to the rest
of your team. This, after three days of familiarity.

You have touched her arms, turned her over,
tucked her in under the plastic sheets,
resisted the temptation to comb her hair,
to flick her withered teats.

You must proceed with the unbuilding,
trim her of the globules
just above her waist, knobs of fat
a husband called "love handles,"

burrow into the rutted tunnels
where her thighs grazed against each other,
slice down her abdomen, now tumulus,
which grew a fetus twice at its core.

If you feel you are turning gray,
or think you are party to a violation of life
even though she chose to have it this way,
didn't want to go bedded in pine,

it will not help to ask what color the flesh is,
how the tissue you hold in the clammy bowls
of your palms feels, or whether you imagine an army of frozen
insects thawed, then crawling the tunnel of your throat.

Soon you will cease to think of this object as woman or wife.
You will discover how things work, get to know each part,
you will learn something important about life:
what it is not.

for Wallace Goldban

Of Pine

What you recalled again and again was the pine forest rimming the river,
      the likeness of pine glazed on the water,
the pine bench on the porch where the farmers rested to tie their shoes
      or have a drink,
sun climbing the pine, the river rising, the old town cut by the river
      fringed with pine,
the path in the fabric of pine like a torn seam and you a thread on pine
      skis lacing the frayed edges,
how you entered and closed a gap.

Last year Sam went back to see what was left, to sit on the porch, to
      walk through the pine.
That the SS had burned the town was no surprise, but he didn't talk
      about the pines, didn't say they howled,
that pines gridded the sky with poles of flame and riddled the wind with
      charred cones,
how the pine needles, limp in the heat, feathered the air with obscurity.
He didn't tell you only the river remains, extending a long arm through
      the village,
returning bare faces of granite stubbled here and there with stirrings of
      green,
places where roots claw deep into damp earth while you sleep on your
      bed of pine,
your pillow flagrant with pine, a bird nested, dreaming in pine.

You Are Like This Where You Are

the one veiled like a bride
the one alone for the first time
the one at the stove
the one supine, a plug in your throat
grammar tongued by earth
the one who presses palms to her groin
the one who wrings her hands at the sink
the one who leaves home and never returns
bereft of a house, bereft of a room
the one who goes after the future
hemmed by hours stitched into skirts
the one who ignites coals in the caves of her eyes
beware how needles shoot into flame
the one who loses the future
the one who blocks felt in a sweatshop
the one whose fingers of air rustle the leaves
the one who survives—the only one
eroder of soil, draper of stone, pleater of wind
your arms of fire circle the pines
the one who smashes the roots
the one who poses with twigs
the one whose spectacles widen her eyes
the one with my eyes, with my brows, with my mouth
the one who leaves Ostrolenka, Chicago, New York
the one who leaves no trace
the one who scales mountains of death
dreamer crushed by the gravel of life
the one who climbs two flights five times a day
the one whose sheets stiffen in the sun
the one who cries when she rinses her hose
buyer of remnants, raveler of fact
riddled with words
namer of days without windows, dusks without doors
the one who slips her arms through the sleeves of the house
bountiful belly, birther of children

the one who sleeps with the stench of his feet
the one whose tongue marbles in her mouth
the one who tries not to think so she fails to remember
the one who never forgets
the one who sprawls jacks on the floor
the one who leans from the window
the one who peers down the street
the one who thinks of jumping
the one who ladles soup at the stove
alone, alone for the first time
for the last time
in the long memory
before arrival
calm in the unruly silence
the generous one
mulch beneath juniper

Lion, Sand, Moon, and You

A lion chances to pass by . . . and doesn't devour
her. There's an effect of moonlight . . . The
scene takes place in a completely arid desert.

Henri Rousseau
Artiste-Peintre

She sleeps in the absence of the world, space
named for beginnings elusive to her in the past,
now announced simply by the next breath,
again and again, the same lung-locked refrain
of a stream winding through charted territory to guard
or confine her, she cannot know. And behind her the lion,

its tail an expansive gesture above the horizon, the long line
of memory, tenderness of an arm flexed against space
as if to stop traffic, though now there is none, or to guard
her, though now she is alone, all the others having passed
without leaving signs in the sand, echoing the refrain
she hears faintly, wind fielding fragments of breath,

clouds dismissed by a graying sky. The feisty breath
of courage and independence exhaled by the pacing lion
snakes around her body. But she is far from the tentacled reign
of cities, the invasions of vegetation of open spaces.
She nears the sleep of all sleep in silence long past
desire or fear, loss or regret, steeped in patience that guards

against the world's usage while it disregards
everything but the journey under the moon through the breadth
of experience. What else is there but the irretrievable past,
momentary present and the bolted door of the future aligned
before her, mysteries squandered: unalterable spaces,
light honeycombed from wave to hill, words dangling, the refrain

of questions skittering like mice in a maze, the disconsolate rain
drowning roof tar, shrouding windows, as if to guard
against dissolution that looms from the first day, then in space
left fulfills its promise, revokes her very breath.
Why, then, is she left with sand, moon, and lion?
Phrases of poetry, perhaps, to evict future and past

from the equation because what has passed
and what is to come does not matter. So, sleeper, refrain
from attempts at understanding or retrieval. Lie here on
this cusp of earth where too often you have been caught off guard.
That will not happen again. In this absence, though your breath
is expendable, you will not mind. In this absence issues of space

are long past your concern or regard,
and the refrain is no longer your breath.
A lion, silent and sure, takes on your space.

Camera Work

Consider the shot corresponds to spirit, a root claiming heaven in a
    speck of soil;
And consider it equals a guffaw in the face of time—
Virulent fritterer of days, flesh, even giant sequoias—; consider it
Emblem, anchor, statement *I have them still*,
Assertion, indeed certainty, a victory is at hand,
That each click   is witness   is testimony   is mirror   is signature   is

Evidence: A man and a woman seated on a bench, two sepia
Mouths on a clean slate: *Look at us, here we are, we swear we will*
Parse nothing but the whole truth. Gravesend Park. Arms entwined, sun
    streaming down
Their physicalities, smiling faces of an afternoon when the world was
    younger
Or more innocent, but even then a place where rhododendron and azalea
Retreat into a horizonless future, keening a bit,

Knowing, as the Greeks did, to step carefully, backwards,
Ogling the past as if it were a companion, a mechanism for
Defense, access to an antidote for the powerful candor of what is upon us
As soon as it has half a chance. There they are. Shirts open at the throat,
    grass
Clipped under their feet, children causing no mischief. Parents perched
On oak planks, looking careless despite the bespoke cut of their coats.
Leaning toward death. Posing still. Now and never. A terrain strewn with
Oughts. So many oughts when time is past and damage cast in the
Rough truth: we rarely spoke, I did not stroke his arm or hold her hand
    when

Foreground was sharp and left nothing to its own or my invention.
As if they fool me for an instant. Death-defiant, deckle-edged,
Drained of being, arrested, detained for an indeterminate sentence, no
    chance for parole,
Engaged, till life do us part, ratifying the inexplicable fact: when we
Sign up, we sign out.

Without

What contrives to strip the antique chest
of patina, the steel chair of black
paint, the unbodied coat of the logic
of buttons? His heart marbles in the crevasse
without breath to fill the figments of its
engineering. It is without . . . The last

words without dwelling, arranged then
rearranged without so much as . . . On the periphery,
at the brink, broaching the sidelines. Equally
devoid, at a loss, deprived of a footprint. The stated
place in the proceedings changed, the seat on the benefit
committee unoccupied, the dismantled plan.

It is to be without . . . Outside the play,
without the task of belonging, when wild gusts
succumb to the grayness of ash and the old lust
wraps its ruins in brittle stalks
advancing now without sun's rewards.
Without welcome . . . another day.

For a long time he has been without the will
to carry on, like putty, limp dough
in the arms of departure, unable to rise to the known
world because it has kneaded him carelessly between
its fingers, rolled him on its marble slab with the heel
of its hand, baked bread green with mold, and stale.

Portrait of the Young Woman Duressed

after Arcimboldo

Dilated nostrils, jagged pits where lips meet,
unplotted maps of desire that lurk in the pores—
these are the faces she must unseat—

tongues unleashed in saber rage,
eyes of clenched fault down the skull's miles,
mouths wrenched open to corridors of caves—

passing access to the useful grave—lids
like brooding shields in the cheek's asylum,
jaws knotted in the ever-needed rigor

of defense. These are the emblems
which make her veer from her days,
as if the body pitched in a different direction

aborts the illusion deployed to answer
the question, as if there could be an answer
in the disposition of one feature or another.

What a bother! This troubling of her head!
Why not beg the question, ignore
the agenda that again, again skirls its dread

tune to upwelling threnodies of fright
locked in the crypt of throat? On curled toes,
knees bent, chest thrust forward, discrete

creature, you must start, you must start—
bare your jaguar fangs; devour your part.

Age

Yes, it is you in the mirror with fine vertical lines along the margins of your mouth, you with skin pleated like Fortuny silk, fingers mottled brown, rising to peaks at brittle joints.

Each day is a gift you parcel with care. Wrapped in the sheet, you wake slowly at 10 a.m., curled on your side in the fetal position that gives your spine relief. You have breakfast—a saucer of cereal with milk, an inch of sliced banana, half a cup of decaf—tidy the bed, dust where dust has rarely been, call Janet, then Rose, make sure their day's begun, as yours.

By noon, if it is sunny, you sit at the pool, discuss the weather, exchange stories about your granddaughter who sings with a jazz band in Paris, her grandson who earns $50,000 per year right out of law school, young couples who carry babies on their backs to rock concerts. You try to understand how time and blood have spun their threads. You try to ignore the ache that resumes its place at the base of your spine.

Later, in the kitchen, before you turn to the TV and your daily paper, you get down on your hands and knees to ease the pain, go fetal again. Above you the domed ceiling emits a warm yellowed light through Lucite tile. You arch your body, press your forehead to the floor. Weightless, you ride the earth while it turns its back to the sun and dark rises from an ancient crust.

Each morning another day, each evening another night.

It is more than you expect.

for Freda Rabinowitz (1902–1993)

Again and Once Again and . . .

Against all odds, and past their prime, lychnis, astilbe, lythrum pitch fresh
     bloom headlong into pale gardens, and
Notwithstanding the dense sprawl, inkberry, beach plum, spartina squab-
     ble for patches of meadow. Frogs churn silt through speechless
     leaves
And clouds in rumpled skirts writhe as the lotus noses skyward untame-
     able desires to break from home.

Phragmite brindles the colorless wind. Bobwhite calls, cries, pealing its
     name—endearments hammering close to (far from?) the
Heft of things. As if to curtail dying—as if to repay a debt—as if he
     grieves, pleads and grieves—as if survival is possible and he must
     not slack off.
Overused, begging the same question, retracing the track, climbing the
     caprice of what is out of reach in the round of
Rounds around the edge of woods, of dawn and dusk and afternoon—
As if he cannot be without this task—this thing to do which is not done.

for Maria G. Fochios

Lifelines

I believe in mystic forces which curdle,
smoke, gyrate around me, worming
into me any time of day or night,
                    just as breath rhymed
with lust led a serpentine line dance through the golem
            molded of wine-dark clay, or the way the dybbuk
set up a disco with flailing lights and
lunatic banners inside the young bride's veins.

I believe inspiration is possible
                    if I pry into the eyes
of yellowed newspaper clippings,
                    if I sail from text to text
through waters which beat meaning into/out of me,
leaving litanies of noun,
                    cacaphonies of cast-off verb,
effusions of adjective on my beach—
                    if I forage for the singular phrase
each syllable revives when given chance
to swim with to/from an unclaimed shore.

And I believe there are archives in the plumage of songbirds—
wood thrush, Baltimore oriole, scarlet tanager—
decodable testaments to migratory lives and places
lived in on occasion, sojourns bearing songs
of fledglings and molted feathers of former times.

And there is courage in self-effacement,
humility in nonexistence, and
endless repetition
in trying to live.

And there are involuntary starts and unused keys

behind padlocked doors of audacities and strangenesses,

and incomplete sentences—

Did they . . . ? Why are . . . ?
. . . I wish on you what . . . There was no . . .

hoping to be rewritten,
lonely in sceneries too faint to be seen.

And there are truisms in habits of plainspeak,
and enthrallments in automata trilling in trees
while *écrivains* write letters in dim light.

And I believe a lion can kill you.

And I believe no one shuffling along the avenue
no one who wakes in a corrugated box,
                no child eating alone
should be unwanted
because they, too, run sentences
into paragraphs of the heart's twilight . . .

I squeezed out big chunks of pure, moist color
and taking my palette knife, I laid on blue, green,
white and brown in great sweeping strokes . . .
I saw that it was good
        and clean
              and strong.
I saw nature springing into life upon my dead canvas.
It was better than nature . . .
                I raced around the fields
like a colt let loose and literally bellowed for joy.

And there is much I would have sung
and many I could have known

had their errands been different,
their weathers more mild.

There are blues I would have used to paint their liquid
names, greens I would have sown to seed their vagrant
fields, reds I would have shrieked to torch
their whited-out moorings in port.

. . . ships in a black storm,
                    vocabularies churning at sea . . .

Notes

"SAPPHO COMMENTS ON AN EXHIBITION OF EXPRESSIONIST LANDSCAPES." I wrote the following commentary for *The Best American Poetry 1989*, edited by Donald Hall (New York: Macmillan, Collier Books, 1989):

> This poem emerged as the result of a conversation my daughter and I had after viewing an exhibition of Expressionist landscapes at the IBM Gallery in New York City. Susan was then completing her degree in fine arts at the University of Michigan and she was having some concerns about her painting. Much of our discussion revolved around art made by males vs. art made by females, and at one point Susan flippantly said something about women needing penises. I couldn't get her remark out of my mind. I also had been wanting to try my hand at Sapphics. I can't remember quite how it happened, but in one of those Daemon-orchestrated moments we experience, Sappho herself came forth as the spokeswoman and put it all together.

"LIMITED VISIBILITY." The epigraph is excerpted from a letter (#506) Van Gogh wrote to his brother Theo on July 16, 1888, in which he takes to meditating about "the eternal question," that is, "Is the whole of life visible to us, or isn't it rather that this side of death we see only one hemisphere?" The complete quotation about an afterlife follows:

> For my own part, I declare I know nothing whatever about it, but looking at the stars always makes me dream, as simply as I dream over the black dots representing towns and villages on a map. Why, I ask myself, shouldn't the shining dots of the sky be as accessible as the black dots on the map of France? Just as we take the train to get to Tarascon or Rouen, we take death to

reach a star. One thing undoubtedly true in this reasoning is that we cannot get to a star while we are alive, any more than we can take the train when we are dead. (*Van Gogh: A Self Portrait*, selected by W.H. Auden [New York: Paragon House, 1989])

The second part of Van Gogh's final sentence remains very true. As for the first part, our space exploration program may well prove him wrong before long.

"DISLOCATIONS." The journey of this poem is the result of a real journey I took in the spring of 1989 to uncover my roots in eastern Europe.

The dissident writer referred to in the section on Prague is Vaclav Havel.

Eva Mettnerova's drawing, also mentioned in the Prague section, is on display in the small museum in the old Jewish ghetto of Prague. The museum is devoted exclusively to the drawings of children interned by the Nazis in the concentration camp of Theresienstadt, a short distance from the city. Eva, who made her drawing at the age of ten, subsequently died at Auschwitz.

"ART-CRAZY OLD MAN." Hokusai (1760–1849), the great, peripatetic Japanese woodblock artist, used at least thirty different names to sign his work and produced approximately thirty thousand pictures. Restlessness, change, and struggle—indeed, an almost divine dissatisfaction—were the hallmarks of his life. Hokusai expressed his dissatisfaction, coupled with an endless optimism, in this excerpt from his epilogue to his three-volume series of woodblocks, *A Hundred Views of Fuji*:

> I have been in love with painting ever since I became conscious of it at the age of six. I drew some pictures I thought fairly good when I was fifty, but really nothing I did before the age of seventy was of any value at all. At seventy-three I have at last caught every aspect of nature—birds, fish, animals, insects, trees, grasses, all. When I am eighty I shall have developed still further, and I will really master the secrets of art at ninety. When I reach a hundred my work will be truly sublime, and my final goal will be attained around the age of one hundred and ten, when every line and dot I draw will be imbued with life. (Quoted in *Katsushika Hokusai*, trans. Elise Grilli, Kodansha Library of Japanese Art [Tokyo and Rutland, Vt.: Charles E. Tuttle Co., 1955])

Hokusai signed this piece with the last name he used: "The Art-Crazy Old Man." Another glimpse of the man Hokusai emerges from his final, prophetic haiku, which is the epigraph to my poem.

"LION, SAND, MOON, AND YOU." Inspiration for the poem comes from Rousseau's painting *The Sleeping Gypsy* in the collection of the Museum of Modern Art, New York City. The epigraph is excerpted from a letter Rousseau wrote to the mayor of Laval, July 10, 1898, offering to sell him the painting.

"LIFELINES." The quotation comes from the notebooks of the nineteenth-century visionary American painter Albert Pinkham Ryder.

The Juniper Prize

This volume is the twenty-second
recipient of the Juniper Prize
presented annually by the
University of Massachusetts Press
for a volume of original poetry.
The prize is named in honor of
Robert Francis (1901–87), who lived
for many years at Fort Juniper,
Amherst, Massachusetts.